# Rosewater

This is a tender collection of gratitudes and love letters to all those beyond binaries and borders. Kaan writes with words I can taste, that resonate deeply with me. They speak to the tangle of desire, familial bonds and where we come from. If you are looking for home, you might not find it here, but you will find someone gentle who will look with you.

- Sabah Choudrey, author of *Supporting trans People of Colour*

We read Kaan's poems and we cried. We don't know if you need to be both Turk(ish) and queer to be moved to tears by these poems but we suspect not.

– Tuna Erdem and Seda Ergul, Queer Arts Projects

In *Rosewater*, Kaan K writes with their typical raw honesty. These poems reject the binary in all forms, while also recognising – even celebrating – the complexities that come with that rejection. By depicting their queerness, their trans identity, and their heritage in all their unvarnished glories, Kaan finds a route to joy and peace through these poems. And in doing so, offers the reader a roadmap to do the same.

- Ben Townley-Canning, fourteenpoems

*Rosewater* takes the witness through a journey and an interruption, moving from home and home, in which home is hazy, sharp, distorted, soft, personal and exposed. There is language to taste and language that leaves the mouth dry. Place becomes emblematic in these poems between a tainted generational space mixed with the familiar London-ness of the Cypriot diaspora. The secrets situated between the speaker and their family highlights the torn diaspora identity - wanting to be connected to land, roots, family, an ancient-ness before conflict (whenever this existed), whilst wanting to live as your freest, truest, playful self in a place where freedom is mistranslated and ambiguous. And encompassing all of this is the realisation that each generation lives a different continuous struggle, which by the end of this collection blurs into one.

- Maria Sophia Christodolou, author of *A disbelief of flesh*

*Rosewater* pulses with tenderness for a Cypriot homeland marked by colonial violence, while asking; what do we do with our love for a diaspora that doesn't necessarily love us back? How do we unravel the stories we have been handed? These skillful poems look for answers in butches who wear pink, crows in Hackney Marshes, a tray of "half tea, half ammunition," the faded top surgery scars of queer elders, a dripping peach offered by a lover, and 'saltwater and strawberry fields.' Sensual and bold, Rosewater is a testament to queer joy, resistance, and love.

- Rona Luo, poet

Kaan's poems ripple and ricochet through you as you read and stay with you long after, lodged like olive pips or stubborn tree roots. I could muse on these words for days on end. Kaan's writing charms and challenges, and they have a unique way of balancing delicacy amongst difficult histories. This book is bursting with pride and bubbling with boisterousness - a blistering liturgy for queer survival. Kaan is a fierce practitioner and one of the brightest voices in the poetry scene today.

- Daisy Thurston-Gent, poet

# rosewater

The land isn't binary and neither am I

By Kaan K // Yas Necati

Playful Pomegranate Press

Printed and bound by IngramSpark.
Typeface EB Garamond.

ISBN 978-1-83654-041-0 (pink cover)
ISBN 978-1-83654-420-3 (gold cover)
A copy of this book is available from the British Library.

For my beautiful sister Leyla,
you are fantastic as the glow of all the stars.
I will love you in every constellation.

For queer and trans Cypriots.
For queer and trans SWANA folk.
For queer and trans Global Majority.
For queer and trans diaspora.
For all of us who have watched our homes cry
because of the colonisers.
And who still dream despite everything.

# Contents

"They invented guns when they couldn't catch birds,
dyke is still the ungrabbable wing"

-    luxx

# Part 1: Green river to Green Lanes

 # Homeland

Homeland
When the sun runs you dry, your plateaus are artichoke bottoms. Cut stems and folding leaves. Spikey inside and out. But with heart tender as an open fist.

Homeland
You are old ruins and new ones. The echo of a whisper in the centre of an amphitheatre. Keys that grandparents will pass onto their grandchildren, promising they will unlock a door that clicked shut sixty years before, bread still on the table, a meal they eagerly wait for you to eat.

Homeland
A village with the biggest vine tree in northern Cyprus. The elder and giant of our border town is older than human conflict. The elder and giant of our border town watches the sea. Watches the rock of a pirate tale. Watches the young with their guns eating stuffed vine leaves by the ocean. Wanting to fill the bullet shafts with grapes, something that will implode.

Homeland
A cricket's song is the only way to feel at night.
I have never stepped certainly on you and I probably never will.
You, in return, ask me to pick a nut from a tree. Ask me to crack it from its shell. Ask me to eat it, right there, unsalted, as street cats lick the dark and hide their paws.

Homeland
You showed me your dead like a hand of cards.
Some see winning hand, some see losing hand. I see a graveyard with
people who died the same age I had my first kiss. Each ace and spade
someone I would have called abla, abi. Whichever "side" they were lost
for. Each king and queen a vine seed reminding us that vine trees grow all
over Cyprus. They do not pick sides.

Homeland
They try to eat your fruit, but we know what to do with the leaves.

Homeland
You never deserved to be a fresh wound of humanity. Blood in our
dolma, blood in our grapes.

Homeland
Still holding British army bases, their planes pollute the taste of our
artichokes.

Homeland
I have never known a night sky like yours, a pillow from all angles, you
held many weeping silently into.

Homeland
Who keeps floating despite being closed in on all sides by sea. Who keeps
holding grandchildren without grandparents. Who keeps the bread warm
on the table for everyone, from every side

 # Cutting my grandmother's hair

my grandmother lost her hair long after she lost her homeland  /  there is
no border on her head  /  i am careful with the scissors, they are like UN
soldiers

and her hands  /  holy on her lap  /  are vine leaves

there is a beach on the border, the fence doesn't reach it  /  i collected
shells there once, shells like ears  /  her hair collapses through my fingers as
sand

afterwards, we will tread carefully  /  tread carefully over  /  over the
mountains they are so delicate  /  over the loss it is so fresh

between my fingers,
her hair falls like I wish borders would

 # Home is who nurses

"Nene, will you tell me again the story of the pirates?"

We might be islanders, but we have pirate blood in our veins. I know, because there once were many pirate ships that sailed these waters to get to an island that was rich in olive trees and copper, not east or west, north or south, here nor there - but a joint, a splodge of glue on the map, a rich, fertile land that grew dreams, that made beautiful promises, that brought people together.

But pirates were still men. And when one notorious pirate's daughter fell sick, of course he did not nurse her, as fathers should, but he left her on that rock just over there.

The rock is green and lush and peeks from the sea like a dragon's head. Waves smash against it. It is close enough to shore that you can almost identify the plants, and far enough from shore that you can't make out the details of the flowers. When I was younger, I used to dream of swimming there, but I was too scared.

He left her, and he said [my grandmother attempts her best rough pirate voice] "I will return in a year, and if you are still alive, I will take you back aboard my ship."

In her sickness, it's a wonder she made it to the shore. Some say she was reckless, others empathised with what little choice she had, some say that the sea extended her hand and carried her with care. She ended up on the lip of this village, where the villagers took her against their chests and nursed her back to health.

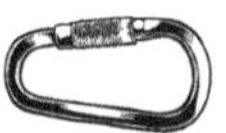

A year later, in strength, she watched her father gawk as he threw his anchor down. He offered her passage on his ship, to be his most treasured guest, to sail the globe like she was the wind.

But she knew who her home was; the green river and its people; those who held her at her darkest. As the man's ship disappeared, they welcomed her back and celebrated her power.

 # Halloumi/Hellim

My village is chewy
And your hometown - a list of ingredients only one of us is permitted to
source

Here, we meet north of the river, ironically -
or not. Garnished in mint. Grilling halloumi on a skewer - sticky summer.
Sheep's milk poured over London concrete

As hellim ages it gets saltier and hardens. What have we kept from each
other?

You are asked to interpret a map
Could I return here
Could I return here with my partner
Both of us looking like *this*
What does it mean to return

To a place you have never been before
 with such a high melting point

What are they eating at the peace talks?

I have visited - somewhere - occupied by human emotions
The grasshoppers are unoccupied by conflict

In both places our origins are less than an hour's drive apart.
But the only language we can speak to each other is our colonisers'

Will you eat watermelon and hellim with me?
I got a day time television broadcast from the queen that said we
shouldn't

Your grandmother must never know you're queer
What does it mean to return?

And I wasn't expecting
And you weren't expecting
A north London park with a squeaky stall selling a place unreachable

I've been meaning to ask
What's your favourite way to cook halloumi?

# My body // the border

**Part I**

1960
- the British "left" Cyprus


Sixty one years later, my grandmother holds half a country on a serving
tray
She serves half tea half ammunition
Her hands are brown and cracked as summer earth
The spot where the river's dried
A division as temporary as the seasons
and such an ancestor that we will never truly know it


//


2021
- my mother tells me, *If the border came down,*
*I would never go back to Cyprus.*
My grandmother still stocks her cupboards full of cans
A makeshift wall, if you like
A makeshift border
Separating her from Britain
She builds Cyprus into the nooks of her home
With tins of heinz tomato soup


//


1996 - 1999
Two children are born
They are presumed to be new
But they are the river as it comes back after dry season
They are named jasmine and night

They will ask why they have been kept quiet around soldiers
They will visit a border town until they digest it
There's something in the soup
Something in their ancestors' cooking


//


I see others
Home sitting on their eyebrows
How do I know their hands?


## Part II


Like the land, I do not belong to anyone.
My body is a border
A scar splits my chest, my stomach, all of my internal organs
My family home is blocking the back of my throat
When I try to state my pronouns
Like the hoca's call to prayer

My pronouns are a call to prayer
My pronouns are what I offer the UN patrol
And the British military bases still in Cyprus
The land is non binary
The land is agender


//


My mother buys me a jasmine plant and I try to help it live
But it wilts in my bedroom

//

My mother tells me, *If the border came down,*
*I would never go back to Cyprus.*
I try to correct her when she uses the wrong pronouns
But my gender is an olive pip stuck in the back of my throat

//

My body sits on a border
Doesn't take sides
My body is a serving tray
Half tea half ammunition
Each half of ribcage a meeting of genders and continents
My hands have short fingernails and scatter olives
They don't look right
They ask
But what if my ancestors were the Erdoğan supporters of their time?

//

My body is bordered
And yet, my body is as unbordered as the land it came from

The land never asked for binaries
The land never asked for borders
The land never asked

//

My sister paints me a picture of the night sky
With full moon
And ceasefire

**Part III**

We are scattered like glitter diaspora
Don't come to us with bullet filled hands
Meet me at your faultline
Then we can cook together

HEINZ
TOMATO SOUP
57 VARIETIES

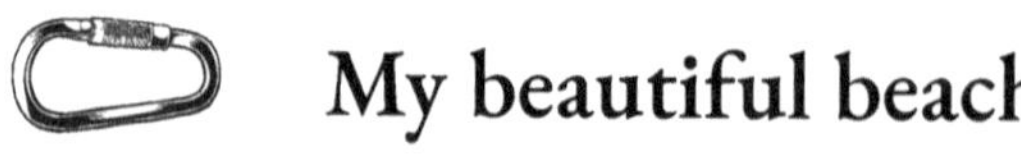

# My beautiful beach

My beautiful beach

I have nightmares about the developers
who have not yet arrived.

I curl into your craters,
left from the bombings.
I imagine myself a cleaner shrimp,
I sip your waters,
they are salty and sugary
and my oesophagus is richer with them

Oh, deep border, oh deep and tender and still bleeding border
Oh dormant conflict. Oh land which holds it

And it is here
I will become queer
And it is here
I will soothe
My soft forming heart

# And then I took a side

The people of this place are rebuilt from rubble
I mourn the gaps in my grandmother's heart, and I forgive her for them
Most of the time

I was raised a Turkish nationalist, and I'm not even Turkish

Turkey is a mother of broken homes and
a father who stuck around, unfortunately

I choose the side of the people of this place, against the people who tried
to snatch it like a pinup moth carcass

I will choose the side of community dinners
I will choose the side of gentleness
I will choose the side of reparations
I will choose the side of the oppressed

I'm standing here asking you to take a side
I'm standing here begging you to take a side

 # I'm afraid of the sea,
# but I want to take you there

I'm afraid of the sea, but I want to take you to it.

Not just any beach, mind you -
this beach -

And when we finally reach it, limbs fresh with dust from the mountain
road down, and sticky enough to catch flies in the heat of the sun,
I want to strip your clothes off, and for you to repeat after me.
For us to amble over rock pools and collapse only once we're breathless
in the heat of the day, in nothing but our skin.
To hold you there, beating heart to sweaty limbs,
home with you.

I have to hide who I am to go home. I don't want to ask that of you.

On this beach, my beach, my favourite place, there are no people.

In the main part of the village, we would risk being the gossip
of coffee mornings, the shame on my family, the attention of soldiers.

But here we could be

Naked
against the vastness of the open sea. To show the ocean our tanlines,
our unkept body fluff, our scarred and healed, marked yet rewritten,
tried and tested skin.

My home is ruptured from here to Cyprus. One foot of mine forever
standing
on the shoreline, exploring the rock pools, getting sand between my toes.

Come be here with me.

# Part 2: Roses

 # Paper Prince

The first trans person I knew is dead /

trans pride 2021 / I listen to Paper Prince

/ I look for her in the folds of my clothes /

at the march we wear flowers / I can't bring myself to hold a rose /

they will say she took her own life / they will say she was trans before they say she played piano / they won't acknowledge who really killed her

/ in the park afterwards there's a fox cub that wanders close /

for all of us treading water / for all of us reborn / for all of us still here / for all of us somewhere safer / for all of us dancing / for the 15 year old who was too shy to talk

I love you

# Staying alive

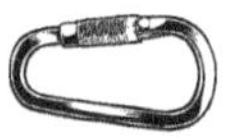

Last night was the first time you saw me suicidal.
You held me and I let you.
Sobbed things into the warm and naked skin of your chest about not
being able to do this anymore and ordering razor blades off of eBay.
Your arms were the only thing.
You held me like hope,
and I don't want to remember any of it.

I wrote my first suicide note at 11.

There were nights I would leave bright red tissues in the bathroom bin
like an alarm.
I feel like this makes me a terrible person.

The morning after
I kiss your forehead and say *I'm sorry*
*I'm sorry I'm sorry I'm sorry*
*I promise I'll never let you see me like that again.*
Liar. I am a liar.
And what I'm really asking is please don't leave me.
What I have is ugly and scary and terminal, I'm sure.
I never thought I'd make it to 23.
But I'm glad that I feel like this means I do have
some things worth living for

 # Part II

I want to be hers whole and completely.
I want not to belong to myself.
Others always do a better job with us than we do with
ourselves - why is that?

//

Obviously, and essentially, we broke up.

Now I study myself and the other queer people I've loved

(all of us were / are mad and traumatised)

We hurt each other because we didn't know how to give or receive care.
We made each other sicker, and sicker. Before we had the tools and the
strength to heal each other.

I forgive us.

And I celebrate the ways we've become beautiful in spite of how many
people want us dead.

# Part twenty seven

,

How can I stay here when everyone like me is dying?

//

When I want to die, I think about my sister. It's one of the only things that keeps me alive.

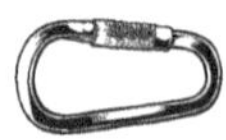

Not every   but most
days I am   a missed alarm
You could hold me to your ear and
still not hear   slow   jazz
playlist or Florence     and the Machine
You could call the IT department
Have you tried turning
them off and then
on again?
Have you tried     anti-depressants?
Have you tried     writing a gratitude journal?
Do you regret it or will you try
to do it   again

In that moment     I was everything but
and nothing more than my forgiving heartbeat.
The beepbeepbeep of the monitor
like a siren   begging   the government for
shorter A&E waiting times
Or a bass line that couldn't wake   me up
I still attempted Christmas.
I still bought and wrapped everyone's presents.
I still went back to work on Tuesday and
applied for more poetry funding and
spent money I don't have on a course that will get me
closer to my dreams and
brushed my teeth while standing
balancing on one leg
and didn't tell my bio family
and held my nibling close
and struggle to cry
and dangled my to do list   in front of
my nose
as if it could do something     for my senses

# Please let me

*For Rose Wong*

Please let me hold some of that for you
Please let me hold you
we are all holding parts of each other, even when we think we aren't

Please let me draw a telephone line that joins the distance
- the first network connecting breathing and not

Please let me be less scared
for the trans kid who asks if it gets easier

Please let me undo words, looks and violence
we have a right to ourselves

Please let me hold something, I promise I won't let it be made a weapon

we would be drowning deeper if it wasn't for you

Please let me hold hope, a piano key, your activism

you were resurfacing
Please let me hold some of that for you

# What it feels like to jump

Even if I crumble.
Even if I hit the ground running like an aeroplane on high impact
or hit the ground softly and bounce back like a boiled egg.
Even if it breaks me -
it's done that enough times already,
the doctor told me not to run again
and here I am marathon training by the
arm of the river.
Even if I shatter -
bones splintered and stranded.
Even if it makes me weaker.
I beat the city. The city beats me.
I want to be out late at night when nobody will watch me, making poetry.
Even if it's dangerous.
Street lights hold me like wax in a candle holder.
Even if I get side eyed by early risers walking their dogs.
Even if it kills me.
I am not reckless with life. This is the only way I know how to feel it.

# The bull

*Thank you, for everything, Ocean Vuong*

I was new then
And naked as the stark white of a horn against a black hedge backdrop
What was I doing here, so far from the arena?
Wet grass clawing between my toes.

To be known better by a bull
Is to step out my childhood bed

To be known better by a bull is to
Trip over groans while I sew the wound back

To be known better by a bull is to
Crack my knees in prayer
And miss myself
And long to be as beautiful as a quiet animal

I dare not touch him
Although my boyhood is stark in his glass oil eyes

# Poems to my names IV: Kaan

I am not a king, or anything really.
I am not a king, until drag kings count.
I am not a king until we abolish the monarchy, and everyone is

I just want something that sounds right when it rolls off my tongue, and
when shouted to me across a busy room, or when whispered to me on a
loved one's chest.

I want a name both hard and soft, rough and warm, metallic and bubbly.
I want a name that feels loving when someone's mouth is around my
cock, and special to a friend when I send them a postcard.

I want a name that says I am alive, that I am doing the best I can, that I
want to love you, that I want you to love me too.

 # Faith

I know I've held hands that have been chapped at the seams, hands that have folded with water or time, hands that have trembled to be touched.
I know my own hands once balled into fists and bruised themselves and they healed from that.
I have seen eyes as brown as the veins of a leaf.
I have known women who have held my body as a tremor on their fingers, left my skin lilac with kisses, asked me questions that I cannot answer.

I know that I have lain in my bed late at night listening to her pray down a facebook video call, both of us with the lights turned out, the fuzzy darkness of a screen and her voice.
I know I have known her voice like a distance and a pen, rewriting touch into my limbs.
In another continent, her hand is on my forearm.

I know I have heard my grandmother pray as I've fallen asleep.
I have heard music that has made my chest, flat with bindings or bandages, breathe like a body that isn't afraid of itself.

I know I have seen boys I grew up with become men who try not to cry at funerals - and wanted to hug them.
I found tickets to Queer Ball in the pocket of the suit I was wearing at a funeral once.
I know I have mourned and danced in the same clothes, the same colours, the same body.

I know that there is nothing I don't believe in, but also very few things that I do.

I believe in gentleness.
I believe in a warm stove and baking scones.
I believe in the leap in our bellies that tells us that we're terrified or
excited.
I believe in saying goodbye *just for now* at airports
and finding those things that make days into daydreams, make moments
into smiles, make hands into interlaced fingers.

# Part 3: You took me in your car / you took me in your arms

# And then Raggi dropped me off at Arnos Grove station

You took me in your car (you took me in your arms)

*How's things with your family?*

Lots of people ask me this, but not how you did.

I looked at your glove compartment. I told you the truth.

You pulled up on a double yellow outside the station. I used to go swimming near here as a kid.

When we hugged goodbye, I hope you felt my thank you through my shoulder blades. They turned soft as mangoes under your hands.

I'm trying not to cry on the train because you get it.
You get it.

# Hackney marshes / Listen.

"Listen"
Language was dropped to us from the trees
we tried to guess what they were saying
watched for the bright green against the bare winter branches
as green as a question mark
maybe they meant for us to overhear them
but probably not

We followed the mud paths
skimmed the water's edge with our boots
left footprints where they didn't
until the paths all around us were silent
and the dark bumped into us
and a single lone human cycled up on the path,
away from our diverted route,
and stopped to look overhead
silhouetted

I have never heard a breath quite so collective
hundreds of voices shaking hands
holding
the space between earth and sky
green feathers meeting the long reach of streetlights
the moonlight bouncing up from the river
the person on the bike was long gone and
we felt our way through trees

On the pitch, lines of goal posts were being watched over
by the far off houses and the skyscrapers
and in the place of kids running, playing 5-a-side,
the crows simply stood.
The deep red hue of a polluted city reached through the fog

 # Marsha

How they pulled up her body and shrugged it off.
As if they'd fished an old jacket out the river and found the closest street
corner to abandon it.
I can see the face of a young gay man as it folds inwards, a scrapping
of unfinished origami.
I feel the crowd say *Marsha, Marsha* with their bones,
and the cops say *time to go home to an already prepared meal and watch
the game.*
I feel the legs sprinting down this street, the crowds as if they're shoving
past me to get through.
There is too much horror.
We love her and there is too much horror.


The Stonewall Inn is busy tonight.
There's a queue to the doorway and people taking selfies
or group photos with the neon sign that marks it.
Pride flags protrude from barriers placed either side of the road.
Back on the pier, we searched and searched for the spot that they found
her -
But there was no sign.
Just bollards painted rainbow colours and a very neatly designed wooden
floor and tables

# Who ever begs in their mother tongue

To be a preacher
Unmuted on leaflets
A megaphone like a sleeping baby
Cradled against warm chest

In the towering flats,
Windows mostly the only audience,
Mothers cook lentils bought in sacks from "international" supermarkets
And the "nationals" go to health food stores
Where they think the doormats are better
And pay ten times the amount for smaller ingredients

The preacher
Stationed in front of the library
The preacher
With a mouth for fingers
Tries to hold every hand and slap every cheek

To be Volkan
Using headphones as a sledge on Wood Green High Street
Making gay jokes
Eating chips as if they were tarot cards
Not yet making gay love
As the takeaway box sits full on the living room floor

To be
To be unrounded
To be a can opener
To be a gentle reminder

To be Volkan's mother
Cooking
Everything she's ever unknown on the stove
She prefers a gas hob but the
Landlord prefers electric

Hands are so full of contradictions
Volkan once spoke with his teeth not his lips

Watch his eyelashes blow like dandelion fairies
Watch his palms opening

The mothers keep stirring
And when the fathers open the doors
The wive's tongues are coins

# Root

in the backyard
under the vine tree
over the sky
trembled and tried
into the party

behind the skin
across the nails with their blunt ends
under the borders
over the fig trees
into the nib of the pen

between the echo
nestled in days spent
opposite futures
downwards and upwards
loo roll and left friends

inside a promise
outside a grown edge
transcending soil
transcending prom suits
transcending the backyard fence

 # Bite

While my grandma watched gay conversion therapy TV shows,
the woman of my dreams came into my days and we cooked aubergine

it reminded me of times when I was young
before Nene knew I was gay
and I would try to help her peel vegetables and she tolerated me even
though I was slow

how cooking is the call to prayer for many Middle Eastern women
how our cultures fold like flour into bread
how she could peel things as well as my grandma
I think that's one of the reasons I fell in love with her
her hands round a knife

the first bruise came like an afterthought
two semi circles holding disbelief between them

my job is to help people out of abusive relationships
but I stay in my own with all of my own advice telling me otherwise
and just as immobilised as anyone would be

It's not that I didn't know that home had teeth
I just never thought they would bite me

My friend said, *anyone who says they would just leave has never known this
before*

# Muhallebi

We tried it with almond milk,
badem and cream,
and when it sat on our tongues it melted like hearts do when they fall
sticky on the roofs of our mouths
warming our insides like a true summer

When muhallebi sets in the fridge, it looks like the mountains on days
they are topped with snow
and we will grab our sledges and our coats
dive like drops of rosewater
transforming milk into an idea of a place we cling to in the backs of our
throats

 # Kurdish coffee

Rich as the seasons
And deep as the cup of a hand

To the women who stir villages like Kurdish coffee

Still surface even if we hold you shaking
Expecting new creatures to emerge

It's a shame you are over as quickly as gossip

# North London balcony

The day is tea
Your fingernails are the violet of sunset
round a billy bragg mug
Beside us, broad beans slow dance
against their canes,
unskilled pole dancers,
learning to sway just for the fun of it

And I think I have learnt that you are a late, but just by a smidge, kind of
person
That you plant tulips on your balcony
and said that you aren't strong
despite lifting my entire body in your arms just moments before
and carrying communities in your wrists and elbows,
all your joints
strong and soft

Okay, maybe you are a late, by quite a bit more than a smidge, kind of
person -
but our kinship is far more exciting than time
I love that you are freehand petals
And thanks to you I can grow my own food
And thanks to you I take a breath between stanzas and sentences

I know that you will nudge me when I'm standing still
and pull me back when I'm running
Your cheeks are archive pages
You always have fruit and water in your home
You are the greatest dancer

In turn, I will offer you a variety of hot chocolates
my ears
my hands for cooking
and a home for your next oil painting

You, the mediator,
the softness of a broad bean
the strength of the stalk

# Part 4: For our shared love of the fruit that falls apart

 # Fruit

There are times my gender feels bitten into

Lips the skin of an apple
plum of the chest
ribs like a fruit basket
I catch slurs in and ripen them
until they are rebellious enough to eat

Oh you dyke,
you queer,
you butch fag
you sissy boy
sweet soft
of a fig's flesh
ripe as sunrise
ripe as what we became
and are still becoming

Andrea Gibson says it hurts to become

*I carry that hurt on the ridge of my lungs*

I love to cook
I love to bake
my gender is sugar
it caramelises beneath my flesh
sweet like giggle
sweet like salt
sweet like days on a lover's chest

 # Q. Masculine

I pointed out where I was from to my ex-girlfriend on a map once. I got it wrong.

My grandfather once said "erkek olacaktı da kız oldu"
They were supposed to be a boy, and they turned out a girl.

*Where am I from?* I am from a question mark.
I am from the times I got asked to leave public bathrooms
I am from healing
I am from becoming

I am also from a place that has the biggest vine tree.
They charge a lot of money for stuffed vine leaves in the UK

I have been unlayering my body and observing it in jars. Sometimes travelling home is getting on a plane, sometimes it is undressing myself, sometimes it is dressing myself.

Downstairs, my grandmother watches gay conversion therapy shows on Turkish TV

Trauma is generational, it passes between bodies long before they are pushed out into the world.
Conflict is generational too -
I hope when we can find peace, we will pass it down.

Downstairs, my grandmother makes dolma,
wraps vine leaves round rice so tight,
places the little parcels between us -
this is her offering
food from her childhood
I wonder what it feels like to carry recipes for more than 70 years

when I am trying to wipe away my past already

I am afraid more than anything of myself and how I will limit my
becoming if I try to be a more acceptable version of *other*

People look at me and ask me what I am.

Do you see my gender?
It is practised
sharp as an insult
tender as an egg shell
curated

Do you see my family history?
It is fragmented
followed by war
mapped out in the food we eat and old pictures full of wounds

Can you remember a time you were brave?

Do you remember your softness, leaking from your pores and between
your fingers?

What does it feel like to catch?

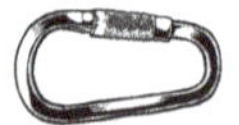

# Peach

in that state between dreaming and waking
you held a peach to my mouth and told me to bite.
you caught the juice as it rolled down my chin
rubbed the flesh into my chest.
i woke up like spring.
you fed my mouth and my stomach and my ribcage.
until i was sticky and wet
And yours

# Purple

yummy

concrete scented rain fell outside your window

we who dyed our hair yellow then lilac

we giggled into each other's jaw lines


the night was delicious

purple with kisses

your lips ripe as a fig straight from its branch

words forming and falling in the gaps opening and closing between our stomachs

as we made love to our friendship and to all we will become, together and apart


The lines in my hands felt like pages

peeling back your layers, your skin so juicy

your back strong as a whisper

we drank each other


my body has been asking me for

your touch so queer in its tender

wondering when we can next ripple into each other

 # Boy lover

I know how this silicone is no longer silicone when you wear it between your legs.
The description of wearing, even, seems silly. Can we wear something that is an extension of ourselves?
I know that when I run my fingers along the sides of your cock you feel it in your belly like I am touching skin.
When I kiss it you tense with pleasure, when I suck it you move against my lips.

That it is your cock. Sometimes there, sometimes not, sometimes wanted by you, sometimes not. But that when it is wanted it is yours and it fits you so well
and fits into me so well.
And I know all of this because there are no words that one trans masc person can say to another that describe the feeling of having something and not, of feeling something and not.
I know that we can treat each other's bodies like we know the other's needs.
This is something that we share.

# McDonalds breakup poem

The time we washed your dog in the bath.
And she looked so miserable yet sat perfectly still the whole time,
Lola the good girl.
And I felt terrible.
And I thought, this is just like a family portrait.

I miss you for the first time at 3:32am in a McDonalds in Birmingham.
Like, properly miss you.
How you introduced me to your family as someone you would be with
for a long time.
How you took my hand and we curled up on the sofa.
How you looked me in the eyes when we fucked and said the word
"mine."
And at the time you looked so delighted and I felt so wrapped in
yoursness
I don't quite know what I'm doing in this McDonald's seven or eight
months later, watching a drunk woman spit on the grey tiled floor,
waiting for my 6am train and writing poetry with shit chips.
I had never been seen so well, my body held so softly.
You called me shnooks.
I called you nootch.
You theorised about our future home and the dark wood furniture
and your kitchen with all the nice jars you would line up on a shelf and
ferment things in.

Once, I would have done anything for you, to be wrapped in you with
Lola under that overhead skylight on your pull out sofa bed.

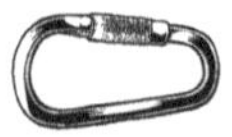

# How do you have sex though?

Straight gals speculate about how we fuck...
and I sit in the corner giggling, thinking wouldn't it be easy to tell them
about your hands gentle on the back of my head
as you sat on my lap and we played tag with my fingers inside of you.
How your head rolled forward to rest on my shoulder and you moaned
my name. How you pressed your lips into my collarbone and bit into me
gently as you came.
Instead I tell them to look up orgasm rates for gay women.

# When butches wear pink

When butches wear pink
even just pink socks
or a pink bow tie
a pink handkerchief tucked into jacket pocket
or hanging from the back pocket of a pair of slacks

When butches wear pink
pink like pink panther
pink like flamingo
pink like a highlighter
pink as the changing moon

When butches wear pink
pink as hot as a burn
or as deep as her lips

baby pink like the clothes they tried to gender us in
rich pink like a piggy bank
pink like the touch of a tongue
pink like the Janelle Monae song
*pink like the colour of your -*
*Baby*

When butches wear pink
that open pink, like pink of a sunset
over a light-polluted city
pink as a brain
pink as an itch
pink as carnival feathers
pink as your name

When butches wear pink

pink of rose water, sweet, sweet,
pink as pink Turkish delight
I want to bite
feel the pink of a kiss
pink of steam
pink boxers under those blue jeans
fuck -
the patriarchy and heteronormativity

When butches wear pink
Amen, amen, amen

# Carabiner

I like the way you feel hooked to my bag or my belt loop,
Heavy.
With a slightly annoying jangling of keys.
Left side, of course.
(If I was a switch would I wear you like a tail? Or a cock?)
I like your cold, smooth metal against my skin.
Leaving chill marks like a change of seasons.
Come clip to me.
Oh.

 # Fag

All that is left of past lovers
is in my fingers when I roll a cigarette

To the women who have been patient with me
I'm sorry
I have never been good at the part where you tuck and roll
I am still learning how to do this better

# Part 5: Ne mutlu transseksüelim diyene

 # Reminds me of home

The woman on the bus reminds me of home. She smells like gülsuyu -
rosewater.
When we were younger, my grandmother used to add a few drops of
rosewater to any cake she baked, so that its smell would be as sweet as its
taste.
At my grandfather's funeral, my mother poured gülsuyu into all of our
palms and we tried to catch it like a dandelion in the wind.
This is how I learned that sustenance and death smell the same, sweet, the
same, sweet smell.

Other things that remind me of home:
Clippers
Strawberries
Brown plants

My earliest memories of home are;
Trying to distinguish bats and owls in the darkness with no street lights
Sitting under a sky so full of stars it was silver with dark blue dots
My grandmothers rolling bread for the clay oven, us getting in the way
My grandfather holding his palm out for a hornet to rest in, under the
limbs of a vine tree
Grapes dangling, jumping to reach the grapes
Watching the soap opera Samanyolu in the evenings
Running round and round the house at night between the small pools of
light from the outdoor lamps
Being told to stop running when the army jeeps drove by
Feeding the feral cats leftover kebap
A man who got a sea urchin stuck in the bottom of his foot and was
showing us what it looked like
The fig tree in my grandparents' garden
The call to prayer waking us up every morning before the light was back.

Shortly after the terrorist attacks outside parliament last year, I was saying goodbye to my grandmother at her home in Wood Green. She cut my path before I could leave.
"Don't tell them we're Muslim," she said.
This is how I learned that no border is a safety net, and no island is an answer.

When I was younger, my grandfather was obsessed with the Turkish version of Deal or No Deal. Var mısın? Yok musun? Erdoğan has banned that now, and Wikipedia.

Other things that remind me of home:
My sister's hair
Army films
A dingy in the shape of a yellow dinosaur
When the UK government said that everyone flying to and from Turkey had to have extra terrorist checks at the airports
When anyone says that North Cyprus is not a real country
Roses
When I say I'm from Cyprus and people ask which side When I say I'm from Cyprus and people don't ask which side because they don't know it was titled with sides

The Turkish flag is red like blood and I don't want to stand under it. The British flag is red and blue like blood and sea and I don't want to stand. I don't want to stand under any flag.

I look for home in everything now.
In the hands of the man who serves me olives in the Turkish supermarket - his brown skin lined as if marked out for fences.
In the radio of a restaurant on Green Lanes, round the corner from my house, with posters in the window advertising Turkish pop stars and

plays about Turkish journalists writing letters from the prison cells where Erdoğan has left them.
In the taste of my grandmother's mushroom börek between my teeth.
Çok tatlı. Like rosewater, it is rich and sticks to the roof of my mouth.

I cannot speak Turkish well. I am ashamed about this.

I look for home, I look for home. On Dalston high road there is a shop called *Cetin Blinds* and a cafe called *Hulya's Buffett* and these are the names of my parents, so I must have found home, right?

But no matter how many times I visit, my home is not a kebap shop near Turnpike Lane.
My home is a distance.
My home is a time of year I always visit in.
My home is an island.
My home is an island not recognised by any other island.
My home is gift-wrapped in barbed wire fencing by 18-year-old boys.
My home is not my home.
My home is a fatally healed broken bone.

One of my earliest memories of the village,
is visiting the graveyard.
Tombstones with names, tombstones without. Tombstones with bodies, tombstones without.
This was your great uncle. He was 18.

Next to the graveyard there are fields of olives, figs, strawberries. This is how I learnt that sustenance and death don't always look the same. The fields will catch droplets of rosewater, and still boys are being conscripted. Still. This is how I learned that no border is a safety net, and no island is

an answer. This is how I learned that more war and more scattering leads to more war and more scattering.

My grandmother's name is Pembe. It's the Turkish word for the colour pink. Pink like rosewater. Pink like the smell of homemade sponge cake with 50p coins hidden inside, wrapped individually in corners of foil.

# Cutting my grandmother's hair II

Now her eyelashes are like little soldiers
Each time she blinks - clink -
their guns tap each other on the shoulder

I miss her childhood, although
I never knew it
I look straight into her eyebrows
bordering her eyes
I want them to be shatterproof
But

# Tambourine

I hope you keep me in the nook at the base of your spine when you leave,
or even better, folded and tucked under your fingernails.
our honesty with the dirt.
this way every time you scratch you will be reminded of us.
not that we are an itch. I would describe you more like a planet and me
more like a ring.

When the Iranian border force took your passport,
I spent hours shaking like a tambourine, unable to sleep.
I wonder if my housemates heard me, clattering against the duvet.
it was selfish of me, thinking about the softness of your shoulder under
my cheek and how I needed that.
I will send you letters, as if that can replace holding your smile between
my palms and the feel of our bodies wrapped naked under a duvet.
I will send you letters, joonam, in a world where a piece of paper can cross
borders, but people can't.

# Green Line (on sanitising language)



*This poem was written in response to the Cypriot embassy in London, who invited me to read my poetry, and then asked me to edit my poems to replace the word border with "green line" (the slang UN title). I pulled out of the event.*

Green is for grass
Green is for go
Green is for walk don't run

Green is for seedlings
Green is for growth
Green is for forest floors of moss

Green is for nature
Green is for freshness
Green is for communication

Green is for dating flags
Green is for approval
Green is for consent

It's a border, let's call it what it is
Soldiers guard its crossing
You cannot walk without showing your passport
If you try you could be shot on sight

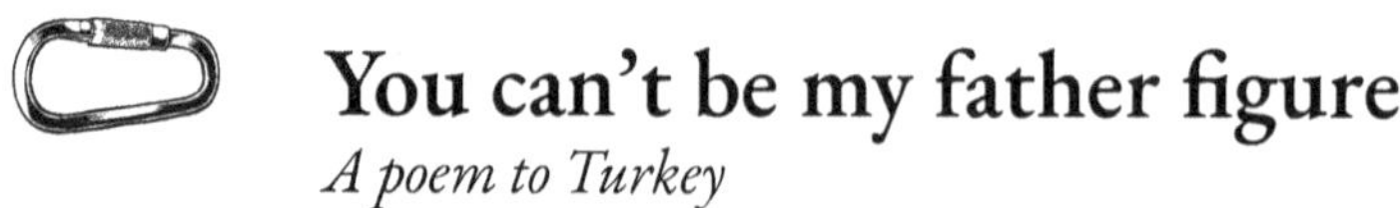

# You can't be my father figure

*A poem to Turkey*

~~One day we will have our own national anthem~~
One day there will be no national anthems

You are not my umbilical cord
You are not my umbilical cord
You are not our umbilical cord
You are not our umbilical cord

# Türk'üm, Doğruyum

Türk'üm.
Doğruyum.
Çalışkanım.
And
God save our gracious queen,
My dog is a good dog
And my god is a good god
And my Allah is a good Allah
Mashallah!
You only paint the picture once
And you only get one chance
Oh when the saints
Oh when the saints
Oh when the saints
Ne mutlu Türk'üm diyene.

 # Oh Turk(ish?) youth!

Your first duty is to preserve ~ queer chosen family ~ and defend forever ~ softness ~.

This is the foundation of your existence and your future.

This foundation altın gibidir.

nE MUTLU TRANSSEKSÜELİM DİYENE.

nE MUTLU EŞCİNSELİM DİYENE.

 nE MUTLU YUMUŞAĞIM DİYENE.

wE STARTED A FIRE IN A BOOK AND IT TURNED THE BOOK INTO MANY MORE COPIES

If one day you have to defend your soft morning kisses, your community hair cutting, your space on the dance floor, remember to breathe deeper than a nationalist's pride.

Your duty is to be dutiless, if you like.

You will find the power you need in your friend's smiles and your own collar bone, your fingers gentle as musicians on your chest.

# Part 6: Homeland

 # Q. Feminine

To the softness,
I'm sorry I didn't write you back.
I promised myself I would never lose you to anyone else.
But I overcompensated

To the sweetness. I put you in a cake and ate it. I listened to my
grandfather repeat over and over *an apple a day keeps the doctor away*. I
found you in a woman who catches my panic attacks as raindrops before
they hurricane

To the saints, I've never been good at holding myself in the palm of my
hands when I pray. Never been good at resting these limbs til they purr.
I caught too many ghosts on my tongue to know what it feels to taste
anything I bake, or anything that anyone else offers me on a plate.

To the sacred, I have caused hurt that has made others shake, and I don't
ever want to do that again.

To the salt, people see me and they ask me what I am.

I am a girl who learned how to cut off her hair.
I am a boy who painted his nails purple.
I am a human who wants to be a lamb.

# Bullet

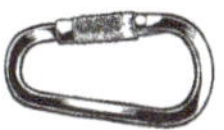

You wanted me to be hard like a bullet.
But I am the soft shell of an egg.
Not the kind stolen and mass produced
for human consumption.
But the kind that holds what's growing
then lets it out.

 # Dreaming myself as a queer elder

Their name is a seed or the rings of a tree trunk, it doesn't matter.
What matters is there's a pot of fasulye in the kitchen, bubbling, enough
to feed 10 or more.
And they are lounging by the fire in their boxers, tracing the faded scars
of top surgery; or climbing a tree in the forest; or making a new chair on
their community woodworking bench.
Their hands are borrowed from generations before
and their thighs are thick with illegible scars, folded under new blankets
of skin and fading tattoos that they really ought to touch up, but it's hard
to find the time.
Amongst protests and cutting hair and ferrying round their niblings
(non-blood and blood) in their pick up truck.

The outside is not healed, but it's getting there.
And inside is full with hot chocolate and morning cuddles and
tenderness.
This is the least they have ever cared about death.

There's always at least one cat and dog about, some rescue chickens and
goats too, under a roof they made from all the joy they collected by living.
The sex is ethereal.
The sleep is easy.

Here they built the unimaginable.
Here they planted many things and watched them bloom and blossom

# Babaganoush

*For Mandy, Myra and Ro*

You pissed on my Kae Tempest anthology and I still love you (all of you, I still have no idea which one of you did this).

My friend once told me about a boy she was dating who woke up in the middle of the night so drunk he pissed in the corner of her bedroom. She dumped him and sent an invoice for a new rug.

Now she has a cat who pees on everything. Her name is Juno, like the Elliot Page character. And of course the cat is here to stay.

My cats are the biggest snobs I know.

I once watched a raw pet food documentary on Netflix that convinced me I would be murdering my own babies slowly if I fed them anything other than fresh salmon I'd fished from the river that morning.

Now I scrape my pennies together trying to afford a tin of baked beans the last two weeks before payday, while those smug bitches munch on Purina one and Sheba gourmet selection in tomato gravy.

Last week, one of them vomited that gourmet food up all over the harness of a tinder date. The little puddle of sick sat right where the cock would slip in.

I tried to be angry but then she looked at me and I forgave her instantly.

The thing is, I have terrible luck with partners.

The last two girlfriends I had were allergic to cats, and this one is a dog lesbian, although I think she's coming around.

Anyone I'm with has to be willing to adopt three children, that's higher than the nuclear family average of 2.4, and be willing to call me exclusively by my gender neutral parenting term, muppa, whenever a cat is in sight.

When my last partner kept sneezing after I first got the kittens, they slept on the bed and we slept on the couch.

There is no love like the love of a cat. When I came out to all three of them as trans like Dana came out as a lesbian to Mr Piddles on the L Word, they continued to do what they always do: cry for food, lick their buttholes and destroy my rented furniture.

My little fluffy angels, fluffas, baby girls, tiny babaganoushes, ain't nobody gonna come before you.

# The village

Pass me that jar of pickled lemon, please,
give me that deep trust
that bone trust
that community dinner
directly into my lungs
belly button trust

Sweet bakes and cooking our grandparents' food together and growing
potatoes and growing with you and howling at the moon and toes
collecting pebbles from the river.
I want to be full as a stuffed vine leaf.

Give me that hand on shoulder rupture-stitching lullaby,
that drag king moustache
that soft care and hard care and caring noodle soup and imperfect
attempts at meeting everyone's core. That unwavering desire to meet
everyone's core.

Hand that protest chant straight into my oesophagus
give me posca pens and ice cream and singing out of tune and dancing to
something that makes you feel alive and hugs as deep as the journey of a
harbour seal.

I want to do life with you.
I want to be with you.
I want to resist with you.
My people. My fruit and vegetables. My village. My garden spades.

# I won't do justice to your palms

or your fingernails

sweet soft and sear of morning
after we threw out our sleep and our separateness

I guess the sun can be here too soon
the night is when I get to rest my head on your thigh
and open my mouth for you

and when I say
I have never been good like this before
I mean it

we deepen into each other
until even the bed frame is queer
and I am a hardened and delicious boy
A delicate boy
A sexy and unhidden boy
in your arms

and the next day,
I am greedy
even on this train, my body wants to open for you
feel your fingers dig me out
cushion your neck in my palm as I press you beneath me

on the ridge of your lips
I will embarrass myself by how much I love you

# The dream

One day we will use the same supermarket
and I'll eat pistachio butter every day and
you'll lick the spoon clean and dirty and

 # Making the bed with you

The bed is not ours
And that's okay

Sheets slump into your chest as you carry them over
I want you to grab me by my corners

The pillows are not ours
But we fold our want around them
Asking
What we need from each other
Tucking it under the duvet
Holding it through sleeping and waking

Our time is a fresh sheet
Over and over
I want to go through many more wash cycles with you

We make the bed
The duvet is not ours but it folds for us

You who can carry me like a river does
And hold me like a memory foam mattress
And touch me like a fresh sheet

I love you
Fabric folding between your fingers like I'll fold for you

The bed is ours for now
And I want to make it again
And again
And keep making it

# Homeland II

Homeland
/ how I miss the touch of you / arm hairs curled and tinged under the strength of your sun / fruit as gorgeous as friendship / you call me like a market stall merchant / you call me with the correct pronunciation / I want to crawl into your belly button, centre of you / I want you to consume all of me but my ears

Homeland
/ how I wish to touch you / again / I would eat your sand / just to know that something inside of me belongs to you / as if you didn't know it already / I want to sit in every sunset pink as a rose flavoured Turkish delight / I want to nibble the sky / swallow salt water and strawberry fields / you are the most beautiful edge I ever saw

Homeland
/ when you show me your neck and shoulders / you are broad from holding their conflict / you never asked to have to be strong and I won't romanticise it

Homeland
What can I do to be with you? / I tried booking a cheap flight but covid / you are an island, expert at self isolating / two halves self isolating from each other

Homeland
/ when I leave, you will bury your sand in the folds of my clothes, so I drop bits of you in my bedroom for months to come /

End

# Playlist

1. *Uzun İnce bir yoldayım* - Tarkan
2. *Please let me (piano)* - Calliope Wong
3. *At this point in my life* - Tracy Chapman
4. *Stray birds* - Rose Cousins
5. *Anchor* - Alys Hardy
6. *Still* - Loyle Carner
7. *I'm new here* - Gil Scott-Heron, Makaya McCraven
8. *Bless the telephone* - Labi Siffre
9. *Yabaal to London* - Bondax, Dur-Dur Band
10. *She wants to be mummified* - Stelios Ilchuck, Yorgos Petrou
11. *Deceptacon* - Le Tigre
12. *Villain Era* - Lady Parts
13. *Let go of the past* - The Tuts
14. *Don't let the sun go down on me* - George Michael, Elton John
15. *My family* - Joan Armatrading

# Glossary

*SWANA* - South West Asia(n) and North Africa(n). A term for what is more commonly known as "the Middle East". SWANA challenges the colonial term "Middle East" that was imposed on us by our colonisers; we ask - Middle of where? East of where?

*Joonam* - Persian, a term of endearment, translating to something like "my love" or "my dear", but much fiercer and deeper. It has many variations across the SWANA region, including the Turkish word "canım"

**Some (Cypriot) Turkish:**

*Gülsuyu* - Rosewater

*Hoca* - Our term for an Imam. It also means "educator"

*Dede* - Granddad

*Nene* - Grandma

*Fasulye* - beans

*Transseksüelim* - I am transgender

*Eşcinselim* - I am gay

*Yumuşağım* - I am soft

*Samanyolu* - a really shitty, problematic Turkish soap opera. We occasionally used to watch it with our grandparents as kids

*Çok tatlı* - Very sweet

# Some context

### Turk(ish*) or Turk(ish?)

Like many peoples who have been messed around by Turkey, I grew up
being told that I was Turkish. It has taken a lot of unlearning to connect
to my Cypriot heritage and family history. However, I acknowledge the
role that Turkish customs, language, popular culture, and influence
has had on my experience, hence the "ish". I am not Turkish, but my
occupiers are somewhat in me.

### Why "Cypriot" or "Turkish-speaking Cypriot", rather than "Turkish Cypriot"?

Cypriot is a political stance. I refuse to accept the fabrication of our
occupiers and colonisers that we are "Turkish" or "Greek"

### Green line

In 1963, a British army general drew a green line on a map of Cyprus, to
indicate where the West believed the cease-fire line should be. This is the
origins of this nickname for the Cypriot border.

### Halloumi/hellim

Halloumi is the Greek name and Hellim is the Turkish name for the
same cheese. At the time of writing my poem about halloumi/hellim, the
EU were in the process of assigning this cheese Protected Designation of
Origin. This means that only halloumi/hellim produced in Cyprus can
be classified and sold as halloumi/hellim in the European Union. Some
folks were unhappy as the EU agreed that both Southern and Northern
Cypriot halloumi/hellim would be included in this status update.

### Why "Kurdish coffee"?

The thing I grew up calling Turkish coffee I later learned was stolen
from the Kurdish people by the Republic of Turkey, and rebranded as
"Turkish coffee".

**Why "kebap" rather than "kebab"?**
Kebab is an anglicised version of the original spelling/pronunciation.
Therefore I use the Turkish word kebap.


**Türk'üm, doğruyum**
A nationalistic oath that all school students in Turkey were required to
recite at the beginning of every school day, up until 2013. I was made to
recite it at my Turkish school in North London every Saturday (although
at the time, I had no idea what it meant). Some poems in the collection
reference this oath.

 # Credits

"Q. Masculine" and "Q. Feminine" were originally commissioned by Homotopia for their Queer Art Always project in May 2020.

"Tambourine" was first published by Mixed Mag in February 2021.

"Halloumi/Hellim" and "Who ever begs in their mother tongue" were commissioned by WiseThoughts Haringey as part of their ACTivate: OurFuture project, July 2021.

"Poems to my names IV: Kaan", "Faith" and "Bullet" were first published by FourteenPoems in *If I were Erol*, June 2024.

# Acknowledgements

Firstly, to Andrea Gibson's "I sing the body electric, especially when my power's out", without which I would not be here today. To Olly, Beth and Toby, for taking me to the hospital.

To Rose Wong, Shay Patten Walker and Alice Litman.

To my daughters/cats, Mandy, Myra and RoBear, for giving me a reason to get up every single day; for sitting on my chest when I've heaved with tears; for all of the deep-belly laughs; for listening to me chat shit basically all day every day; for moving across the country with me when that was my dream, not yours; for your toe beans (and occasionally giving me the joy of touching them); for forming the triangle of protection around me on a regular basis; for all the times you've slept on my pillow and I've woken up and nuzzled my face into one of you; for sprawling out on drafts of this book and my keyboard while I've tried to write/edit; for being my little fluffy angels.

To my beautiful sister Leyla, my favourite person in the world.

To my friends and partners - the loves of my life, particularly Jenni, Angela, Elena, Jess, Deb, Sian, Hannah, Oana and Kit, who have been close by while I've written this book. I couldn't think of a better reason to write than knowing it makes you all proud. Having you all as my family is the best poem I could ask for, and I hope I can keep living it.

To my aunties, elders and guides; Lyn, my NMP3 family, Laura, Tuna and Seda, Nontekozo — and Raggi, oh Raggi <3 (and your cat Taro of course).

To my youngers, inspirations and teachers; Aaliyah and Zaara, Ziya and Mika, Lyra.

To all the people who have helped put this book together: Bea Robinsmith, Olly Cameron, Elena Blackmore, Yorgos Petrou, Florenza Deniz Incirli, Rayanne Chami, Debbie Luxon, Beth Maiden, Jilna Shah, the Dyfi Valley queer writing group. All of the fantastic artists, who you can read about below. To Leilah Jane King for the poetry mentoring. To Abby and Kev. To Arts Council England, and Arts Council Wales (fund the arts!!). To MOMA Machynlleth for the exhibition that will accompany this work. To Angela Christofilou for photographing me like only a friend can.

To London Queer Writers, I miss our monthly open mic nights. To Spoken Word London for welcoming a shy teenager for the first time to the stage. And to our short-lived London POC writing group: Rona Luo, Kyla Jardine, Ash Li, Parissa Ebrahimi and Rayanne Chami - some of the best poets I know. I'm putting your full names here so people will look out for you.

To my Cypriot and SWANA inspirations, icons, co-conspirators, fellow queer and trans dreamers. I am me because you are you. A special mention to Yorgos Petrou, Florenza Deniz Incirli, Leo Farley-Stamadiades (Aphrodite/os), Laz Lightning, Sara Bahadori, Ali Taherzadeh and our honorary Beatrice-Lily Lorrigan. To Pezevengi, to United by Pride. To Dean Atta who I once approached gushing and completely embarrassed myself. To beyza ozer for "fail better". To lisa luxx for "Fetch your mother's heart" and the gorgeous poem "for a subculture to resist capitalist co-opting it must remain impossible to define".

To the people who are Cyprus to me, some of whom are in these poems: my grandparents Pembe, Hakki, Necati and Gulten, the strawberry man and strawberry woman, Meyrhem Teyze and the village that helped raise

me. To my parents. Mum, I know we have our differences sometimes but I love and cherish you.

To the local drag community where I live and to my queer chosen family here in the Welsh countryside. You know who you are and I love you.

To Claire and Jon, for welcoming me at Christmas and always. To Lucy for the yearly card-making.

To Ilaj and Neus for holding me when I was sick and giving me space in your home to heal and to edit this book.

To all of my beautiful co-conspirators across the years, for your wisdom, care, beauty, and for putting up with me writing this alongside the things we've been building together.

To the folks who reviewed the book before it hit the shelves: Sabah Choudrey, Daisy Thurston-Gent, Sophia Maria Christodolou, Ben Townley-Canning and Rona Luo. It is an absolute honour to be read by you.

To all of the spaces and people that have taken me along this creative journey, and the places this work has appeared before, particularly FourteenPoems, Queer Arts Projects, Turkish Delight, Homotopia, Queer Newham, Wise Thoughts, Camp Trans and the NewBridge Project.

To North London, to Green Lanes. And lastly to Cyprus; to kumlu deniz, to the sea life, to the land.

# About the artists

**Elena**
*page 5, 67, 78*

Elena (she/they) is an honorary Mancunian living in beautiful green Cymru, loving on all the textures of the hills and the clouds and the sky. She's a collage artist, spreadsheet-lover, parent, facilitator, Taurus sun / Leo rising.
Find more of their work at elenatayo.my.canva.site


**Ayshe-Mira Yashin**
*page 10*

Ayshe-Mira Yashin is an artist and tarot reader currently studying Illustration at Camberwell College of Arts. Her art practice primarily consists of linework illustrations, risograph printing, bookbinding and tarot. Her work centres around ecofeminism and witchcraft, often exploring queer and matriarchal goddess archetypes from her ancestral regions in the Eastern Mediterranean. Her art has been exhibited in the Courtauldian's "Tongue in Trees", at the IMT Gallery with Naturally Not Binary, in "Do You Buy This?" at Ugly Duck and in "Manifestations" at NIMAC.
Instagram: @illustrationwitch

## Leo Farley-Stamadiades
*page 15, 41*

Leandros Farley-Stamadiades is a multi-disciplinary Cypriot British artist based in London, whose work focuses on the queerification of Cypriot culture and the revival of traditional practices through a queer lens.
@aphroditi.os

## Rony Junior
*page 27*

Rony Junior is a multidisciplinary artist, writer, and queer film programmer, with a background in art direction and curation.
Instagram: @ronydaccache

## Sara Bahadori
*page 42, 47*

Sara Bahadori is a queerfeminist photographer and political educator on intersectional climate justice based in Cologne, Germany.
Website: sara-bahadori.com // Instagram: @saraisaveganphotographer

## Yara Mina
*page 50*

Yara is a Lebanese/Cypriot/queer multi media artist (she/they).
Instagram: @yaram1na

**Sarah Wilson**
*page 73*

Sarah is a multidisciplinary artist who works with music and visual
media. From an early age her work has been political, exploring themes
of identity, race and sexuality and she has a keen interest in the natural
world. Her work has been exhibited in art galleries such as Ikon
Birmingham and BMAG and she has worked as a facilitator encouraging
disaffected young artists for many years.
Instagram: @sarahtiptoegirl // soundcloud.com/user-309939349

**Jess Poyner**
*page 81*

Jess Poyner (they/she) is a trainer, facilitator and activist who has been
working in social justice movements for over a decade, currently based
between mid-Wales and Berlin.
They have worked on youth empowerment and peer sex and drugs
education, before moving into feminist and anti-racist organising in
2014. From 2019–22 Jess worked for Good Night Out Campaign
coordinating, facilitating and designing workshops on preventing and
intervening on sexual violence in music and entertainment communities.
Jess is part of the abolitionist collective Cradle Community through
which they organise workshops on self-accountability, active bystander
training and prison abolition. As part of Cradle Community they co-
wrote *Brick by Brick: How we build a world without Prisons*, Hajar Press,
in 2021. Jess also explores Black prison abolitionist politics through
speculative fiction. Their short story *Day 62 on Earth*, was published in
*Abolition Science Fiction* in 2022.
In their spare time they enjoy using watercolour, lino print and oil paints
to express themselves.

# Kaan K

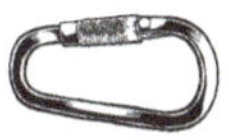

Kaan K, born Yas(emin) Necati, is a writer, drag king and workshop geek. They were gal dem's gender columnist and their chapbook, *If I were Erol*, was published by FourteenPoems in June 2024. They grew up in North London and now live in mid-Wales with their three extremely fluffy cats. *Rosewater* is their first full poetry collection.

kaank.co.uk
@dream.with.kaan

Cyngor Celfyddydau Cymru
Arts Council of Wales

ARIENNIR GAN
Y LOTERI
LOTTERY FUNDED

Noddir gan
Lywodraeth Cymru
Sponsored by
Welsh Government